PRAISE FOR KICK IT UP A NOTCH MARKETING

"Al and Jerry hooked me in the first chapter. Read this book and propel your business to the next level."

–Sande Ellis, Remax Realty Group,
Top 100 Agents in the US, Ft. Myers, FL

"Marketing is the key to building your asset-based real estate business, and this book gives great marketing ideas."

–Linda McKissack, Millionaire Real Estate Agent
and author of Presentation Mastery for Realtors

"Well done! I wish this type of information was available when I started in the real estate business. This book removes the error factor and puts your success on the horizon."

–Dr. William Barnes, Broker, Gracious Living Realty,
Providence Forge, VA

"Al and Jerry share all their secrets for successful marketing. By reading this book, implementing its marketing strategies, and putting key issues into practice, you will generate more business and enhance your real estate career."

–John H. Smith, Owner, John Smith Real Estate Group,
Elizabethtown and Hershey, PA

"Powerpacked with ideas! For those who are more seasoned in the real estate business, this book is a great reminder of the basics we have forgotten. For those who are new to the business, it's a step-by-step guide to creating great marketing habits for your unconditional success."

–Lillian Montalto, Lillian Montalto Signature Properties,
Andover, MA

"From the first steps of writing a marketing plan to leveraging fusion marketing, Al and Jerry have helped me reinvent and strengthen my real estate marketing strategy."

–Zac Pasmanick, The Zac Team,
Atlanta, GA

"Perception is perceived reality, and marketing presents the perception to prospect. Kick It Up a Notch Marketing is right on target to continually support an agent's business and mindset to grow into a profitable real estate empire."

–Char MacCallum, President,
Char MacCallum Real Estate Group, Inc., Olathe, KS

Kick It Up a Notch Marketing

25 High Impact Marketing Strategies for Real Estate Professionals

Al Lautenslager

&

Jerry Pujals

06 07 08 09 10 HH 5 4 3 2 1
First Edition
Printed in the United States of America
ISBN 10: 0-9-9774659-3-4
ISBN 13: 978-0-9774659-3-4
Bus054000 Business & Economics / Real Estate
Library of Congress Control Number: 2005937906
$24.95 U.S. Funds
$ 28.32 CAN Funds

Requests for permission to make copies of any part of this work can be made to:

Cameo Publications
478 Brown's Cove Road
Ridgeland, SC 29936

1-866-372-2636

Cover and interior design by Cameo Publications, LLC.

Dedication

From Al Lautenslager:

*I have a personal mission to help as many small businesses and
organizations as I can through my speaking and writing.
Those real estate professionals who benefit from this
are included in this dedication.*

*This book is also dedicated to those who combine
preparation with opportunity.
May this volume contribute to that preparation so you are ready
when the door of opportunity faces you.*
Good luck!

***

From Jerry Pujals:

*To my wife, Susan,
and my children, Dustin, Trent, Alanna, and Little Jerry.*

*How fortunate can one person be to have a family that stands
beside him and supports him every step of the way.
I love you all very much!*

Contents

Acknowledgments... xiii

Introduction... 19

High Impact Strategy Number One:
Get into a Marketing Mindset.....................................25

High Impact Strategy Number Two:
Develop a Marketing Plan..29

High Impact Strategy Number Three:
Define Your Competitive Advantages............................37

High Impact Strategy Number Four:
Identify Your Core Services 41

High Impact Strategy Number Five:
Define Your Target Markets 45

High Impact Strategy Number Six:
Figure Out a Client's Lifetime Value............................49

High Impact Strategy Number Seven:
Start Networking... 51

High Impact Strategy Number Eight:
Develop a Referral Strategy..57

High Impact Strategy Number Nine:
Be Consistent with Your Commissions Structure....... 61

High Impact Strategy Number Ten:
Offer a Guarantee..**63**

High Impact Strategy Number Eleven:
Do Some Online Marketing...**65**

High Impact Strategy Number Twelve:
Invest in Advertising...**71**

High Impact Strategy Number Thirteen:
Send Direct Mail Pieces..**75**

High Impact Strategy Number Fourteen:
Write Sales Letters..**79**

High Impact Strategy Number Fifteen:
Create Brochures..**83**

High Impact Strategy Number Sixteen:
Do Some PR..**87**

High Impact Strategy Number Seventeen:
Develop Your Expert Status...**91**

High Impact Strategy Number Eighteen:
Send Thank You Notes...**93**

High Impact Strategy Number Nineteen:
Do Some Direct Sales...**95**

High Impact Strategy Number Twenty:
Consider Telemarketing...**97**

High Impact Strategy Number Twenty-One:
Do Some Speaking 101

High Impact Strategy Number Twenty-Two:
Develop Multiple Hooks...................................... 103

High Impact Strategy Number Twenty-Three:
Work Your Database.. 105

High Impact Strategy Number Twenty-Four:
Practice Client Attention.................................... 107

High Impact Strategy Number Twenty-Five:
Get Active with Fusion Marketing...................111

Appendix 115

A Quick Word About Turbo Charging Your
Marketing Efforts.. 117

A Quick Note From Al 119

A Quick Note From Jerry 121

Sign Up For "Market For Profits" Free E-zine........... 123

Quick Start Action Sheet 125

Free Special Report #1 127

Free Special Report #2 131

About Al Lautenslager....................................... 137

About Jerry Pujals.. 139

ACKNOWLEDGMENTS

From Al Lautenslager

As with any writing venture, it takes a team of support. My best teammates are my wife, Angela, and my daughter, Allison. Thanks for your support and unending love. I love you both.

I would also like to acknowledge the passion and spirit of my co-author, Jerry Pujals. His hard work and vision have helped make this book a reality. Thanks, Jerry.

One last word of thanks to Jay Conrad Levinson. Jay had faith in me when we launched the *Guerrilla Marketing in 30 Days* book early in 2005 and continues to be a friend, mentor, and inspiration. Thanks, Jay.

From Jerry Pujals

Writing a book is a huge undertaking that I could never have done alone. Therefore, I wish to thank the following people for helping me make this dream a reality.

To my wife, Susan. Thank you for being you and for always sticking by me through thick and thin. You have always believed in me, and I am so grateful for that. I love you.

To my children, Dustin, Trent, Alanna, and Little Jerry. Thank you for being so supportive and for being my incredible group of cheerleaders. I am so proud of each of you and grateful for you every day. I love you to the moon and back.

To Greg Dunton, my best friend in the world. Thank you for being an incredible business mentor. You have taught me what wealth really is, and that becoming rich is not about the destination; it's the journey. Thanks for helping make the journey so much fun!

To Hilda Hensley, another of my best friends in the world. Thank you for being a great sounding board and voice of reason.

To Gene Ciabattari. Thank you for teaching me the power of simplicity. You have always been there for me and are always encouraging me to reach for new heights. I could not have asked for a better financial coach and great friend. I will always keep learning from you.

To Angela DeFinis. Thank you for sharing your incredible wealth of information and experience. You have introduced me to so many influential people. My dream and new chapter would not have come together as fast as it did without you.

To Michael Lee. Thank you for all your selfless acts with the members of the NSA. Without your help, suggestions, and willingness to share, I know this project would not have been completed as fast as it was.

To my office staff, Carrie Wilson and Dustin Pujals. Thank you for being so supportive and working with me through all my ideas, no matter how farfetched they may be. You're the best.

To my office manager, Doug Fowler. Thank you for taking a chance on me. When I told you I was going to sell 100 houses a year even though I had no experience, you believed in me and gave me a shot. Thanks for always allowing me to expand to new horizons.

To Robin Rose. Thank you for always giving me a platform to express myself and help other agents improve.

To my personal real estate training coach, Tony DiCello. Thank you for teaching me how to become a better coach. You helped me understand that part of being a great coach means being a great listener. Thanks for listening.

To Patricia Fripp. Thank you for all the inspiration through the years. You have helped me directly and indirectly through your coaching and the way you do business.

To my cousin Robert Rodriguez. Thank you for being supportive and willing to listen at any hour. You're like a brother to me.

To Brian and Christy Rodriquez. Thank you for being part of the mastermind group that helped me realize it was time to write this book.

To everyone at Cameo Publications. First, to my editor, Dawn Josephson, thank you for keeping me on schedule. You have a way with timelines that I've never seen before. Your ability to always under-promise and over-deliver never ceases to amaze me. To Dave Josephson, the marketing innovator, thank you for all your hard work with the branding of me and my book. We're the two most different people in the world, but we're alike in many ways. I appreciate our relationship because you really "get" me. To Gail Westerfield, thank you for your follow through on every detail. You are a great team!

Finally, to everyone who has ever touched my life by helping me to believe without limits. A piece of each of you is always with me. Thank you for sharing this journey with me.

KICK IT UP
A NOTCH MARKETING

INTRODUCTION

"I'm really focused on operating my real estate business and making sure all the right things are getting done: pre-qualifying buyers, taking care of anxious sellers, filling out all the proper forms, and generally doing all those things to satisfy clients. I really don't have time for marketing. I'm a real estate professional, not a marketer. Do I really have to market my real estate business?"

Sound familiar?

When we first received this question, we had to re-read it to make sure this real estate agent was really asking if he should be marketing his business. To us, it's obvious that all real estate professionals should be marketing all the time, but most agents simply don't do it.

Most real estate agents and brokers are really in the client satisfaction and lifestyle business, and as such, that's where they spend the majority of their time. Think about it…Much of what you do is to give clients more peace of mind of where they live and the quality of life that they desire, by providing the right home, house, and location.

With that in mind, why, then, should a real estate agent/broker market, and how can real estate professionals be involved in marketing if they are worried about hundreds of other business ownership details?

First, we'll answer the "why." To state the obvious (which we're finding out isn't the obvious, so pay attention) all real estate professionals need marketing to help them achieve the visibility required to get noticed in their marketplace. This visibility leads to more prospects, converted to more clients, converted to more profits. That is the formula for staying in business. So by deduction, real estate agents need marketing to stay in business.

Let's face it. Clients come and clients go. Sometimes they leave because of us, sometimes because of them, and sometimes because of factors beyond the control of either. No one can always predict or forecast when or why a client will leave.

In order to safeguard against attrition, you need to always have new clients coming in the door to replace those who leave. You must always be gaining new listings and closing new sales for an ongoing business. Since not everyone you market to will become a client, to get those new clients you have to continually put your message in places where prospects will see it, and not just one time. It must be continual.

Marketing is made up of many things done over and over and over. Without this repetition, you have no new clients to replace old ones, and you soon enter what is known as the "death spiral" for your real estate business. But this "death spiral" is not an option for you!

Imagine you are successful getting your fill of clients, listings, and sales, and you get busy fulfilling your clients' every need. This is a good thing; however, you must continue to pay attention to your past clients and prospects. **Lack of attention is the number one reason clients leave and never return and is the number one reason prospects won't go forward with you.** If you get busy, how can you stay in touch with your most valuable clients and prospects in a periodic enough fashion?

The answer is marketing!

Different marketing vehicles can help you stay in touch with your clients and can show them that you are paying attention to them. For example, you can send thank you cards, special offers, tips and techniques, newsletters, etc. This is all considered marketing and is a way for you to stay in touch without being there in person. When your marketing results start paying off, you will soon be saying, "Thank goodness for marketing."

Now, let's say that your business is growing and you are branching out. Who will list and buy from you? The answer is obvious: Past clients as well as new ones, but they won't do either unless they know about you.

Marketing lets them know about you, your services, and your company.

Service announcements, press releases, newsletter ads, advertising, and just sold/just listed mailings are only a few of the marketing vehicles and tactics you can use to alert prospects and past clients to your new products, services, and activities.

Marketing, once again, saves the day, enables you to pay attention to your clients and prospects, informs and educates them, and causes them to eventually empty their wallets into yours.

In the world of guerrilla marketing, the rule of thumb is that you should spend sixty percent of your marketing time and resources on current and past clients. In the real estate business, this is mostly past clients.

You should spend the remaining thirty percent on new prospects, with ten percent being spent universally.

All of this spending should happen simultaneously. You need to keep your prospect funnel full while continuing to convert prospects into paying clients.

Current and past clients represent your best prospects. That statement is so important that it bears repeating: Current and past clients represent your best prospects.

Why? These are the people who already know you, have trusted you, and have confidence in your company, products, and services. These are people you have already started a relationship with. These are the people who have had a good experience with you already.

All of these factors increase the probability of someone buying from you. The fact is that if someone doesn't know you or hasn't had any experience with you, you're going to invest more time and money to convert that person to a client. Let this knowledge drive your marketing message, your marketing tactics, the way you deliver them, and the frequency in which you communicate.

Understanding this basic difference of guerrilla marketing can keep your marketing costs down and increase your return on the dollars you spend. Guerrilla marketing emphasizes profits, not just top line sales. Yes, both are nice, and that's why you need marketing.

Now that you know why you need marketing you're probably still wondering about the "how" question we posed earlier: How can real estate professionals be involved in marketing if they are worried about hundreds of other business ownership details? In other words, how do you fit marketing in, where do you start, and what do you do next? Do not despair. That's where this book comes in.

You are about to learn marketing strategies that have proven successful in other industries. These are things that work—things that drive clients to your business.

You will be digesting lots of information here. You may not be able to apply it all. In fact, you may not need it all. Parts of this book will work better for you than for other agents. And that's okay. The key is to take what applies to you and then implement it.

To make it easier for you, as you go through this book, highlight those things that you:

A: Understand;

B: Like;

C: Think will work for you;

D: Think your clients will like.

Then prioritize these, identify next steps for implementation, and do them.

— Above all else, be prepared to take action. —

If you don't take action, no one gains, including you. If this book merely sits on a shelf, it is just taking up space. Don't be a "space taker upper." **Be an action oriented, intentional marketer.** Think marketing all the time and you will soon be thinking profits all the time.

This book is just one of many resources available to you. Throughout the book we will identify more resources for you. Take advantage of these. Make a list of them and take a look at them. Some will be books; some resources will be online and digital. If you have any questions as you read through these, please feel free to e-mail us at **al@market-for-profits.com** or **jerry@jpsalessystems.com**. We will do our best to answer your questions or find the answers to them quickly.

Rest assured that no matter what your situation, whether you're a newbie fresh out of real estate school or a veteran agent, you'll find something in this book for you. Don't fret over which marketing strategies to do. Just pick the ones that make sense for your situation and do them.

Just start by doing something. We can't emphasize this enough. Things are in your favor in a bigger way if you take action.

Happy Marketing,

Al Lautenslager
www.market-for-profits.com
and
Jerry Pujals
www.jpsalessystems.com

HIGH IMPACT STRATEGY NUMBER ONE:
GET INTO A MARKETING MINDSET

In order to accomplish something you want, you must have the proper attitude, the proper mindset, and the proper game face on. It goes back to the old saying that if you always do what you have always done, then you will always get what you have always got.

If you purchased this book and are in the real estate business, then you certainly want to do better than you have in the past.

Wishing for it won't make it happen.

In the introduction we mentioned, "Be prepared to take action." That's a good start to your mindset. You must believe that marketing is a way to help your business, a way to improve your current situation, and a way to achieve the success you dream about.

We're not going to spend a lot of time on mindset, but it is as important as the other strategies in this book.

Part of establishing your marketing mindset is setting your marketing goals, stating that you will think of your business as it relates to clients and prospects all the time, and thinking about the benefits you offer.

On top of all this, you will think all the time about how to communicate information related to the benefits you offer and how you satisfy clients. That's a mindset.

Think marketing all the time.

For example, when new people contact you to do business, you will automatically ask them how they heard about you. That's the simplest way to measure your marketing efforts.

Another example is always thinking about why clients should choose you over your competition. Yes, we are going to get to benefits, competitive advantages, and special offers, but for now you are shaping your mind. You are conditioning yourself to eat, sleep, and breathe marketing in everything you do. It's like the professional golfer who always makes the same swing time after time. Like the swing, your mindset will be automatic. You'll get to the point where you don't have to think about it as much.

Another part of having a marketing mindset is doing something marketing related every day. This could be writing a thank you note, working your database, prospecting, planning a referral program, designing an ad, surveying a client, sending out postcards, or doing one of the many marketing initiatives you will come up with by reading this book.

> **Have a marketing goal to do three to five things per day related to marketing.**

Each day you usually check to see how many inquiries came in. You usually check the amount of cash in your bank account. You usually check to see how many people asked about your current listings. You usually make sure that the proper administrative support is in place. You do a lot of things already automatically as a matter of course. Go ahead and add marketing to this.

We know of one real estate professional who posts a big red M on his door when he does his marketing for the day. He lines up his Ms much like pitchers line up Ks at a baseball game, or much like a scorekeeper marks another tally mark on his scorecard.

Once you start your marketing, make a checkpoint on your calendar for one month, three months, six months, and one year to make sure you are continuing your marketing and at least continuing your marketing mindset.

Without the proper mindset you will proceed aimlessly. You will be aggressive some days, and other days you will let something else take over your work schedule. Planning your work and working your plan is so important in the world of marketing, and keeping it on the top of your mind (much like you want your marketing message on the top of your client's mind) is your ultimate goal.

Keeping this marketing mindset will be easier on some days than others. On the tough days when it seems like someone else is controlling your schedule, you must persevere. During those times, say the following out loud:

"I will do marketing no matter what happens today, and I will look forward to doing more tomorrow. Without marketing, my business has less of a chance to succeed like I want it to."

Strategies to Kick Your Marketing Mindset Up a Notch:

1) Keep a marketing journal.

2) Check off on a calendar each day you do something marketing related.

3) Plan and do what is realistic for you emotionally and financially.

4) Tell others that you are now marketing your real estate business, and publicly announce a few goals. This will really hold you accountable.

HIGH IMPACT STRATEGY NUMBER TWO: DEVELOP A MARKETING PLAN

Since you're reading this book, your mind is obviously set on marketing your real estate business. Now it's time to get to work. Enough of the soft stuff. Let the rubber hit the road, starting now!

Planning is the first step.

We recently watched a golf tournament, and the winner said that he won because he was able to execute his game plan. Later we watched a baseball game, and the head coach of the winning team stated that their plan came together.

Hmmm. Every time we hear of someone reaching a goal or someone attaining success, we also hear mention of a plan that worked. There must be something to that planning.

In fact, there is! People in a variety of situations have attained many successes by laying out a plan and then executing it. Now it's time for you to plan your marketing.

We choose to use seven sentences to formulate the basis of a real estate marketing plan.

Sentence one:
What is the purpose of your marketing?

In other words, what do you want people (prospects and clients) to do as a result of your marketing?

With your marketing, you will be sending out many messages, information about products and services, your identity, and much, much more. All of this is designed to give you "top of mind awareness" with your prospects. That is, you want them to think of you as the only real estate agent who can take care of them.

Once they need what you are offering and they remember you from all that marketing you did, you want them to do something. Sure, you want them to list with you and hire you as a buyer's agent, but what specifically do you want them to do? Call you? Send in for information? Visit your web site?

The purpose of your marketing is to have your prospects react to your marketing message by _____. You fill in the blank.

Sentence two:
How will you achieve the purpose of your marketing, concentrating on your benefits and competitive advantage?

You will achieve the purpose of your marketing by emphasizing to your prospects and clients the benefits you offer with you products and services.

The important word here is "benefits." Notice we didn't say "features."

Here's the difference: Being a real estate agent since 1980 is a feature. The benefit is that if you have been around that long, you are likely going to be around in the future when your clients need you. So you are a reliable source of supply.

Being a member of the $30 million dollar club is a feature. The benefit is that because of your past success of selling homes, you will have future success.

Please don't say that the benefit of working with you is that you have the best service in the industry or in the area. Don't say that your quality of service is by far better than the competition. And never ever state that one of your benefits is that you have the lowest commissions in the business.

Good service, good quality, and a good commission structure are givens in today's real estate business. Everybody says it, so it no longer stands out as a benefit. Don't fall into this trap. You can think of so many other reasons why your prospects will want to list with and buy from you.

When thinking of benefits, think, "What's in it for my prospect?" Remember, they don't care about your features. They simply want to know what's in it for them.

The benefit you offer your clients and prospects—the thing your competition doesn't offer—represents your competitive advantage.

The more competitive advantages you have, the better off you are. By offering your competitive advantages and your benefits, you will achieve your marketing difference.

Sentence three:
Who is your target market?

Okay, now pay attention. "Everybody" is not a target. Anybody who wants to buy or sell a home is not your target. You are more than just an order taker. That's why the purpose of targeting is to design the proper marketing message with the proper benefits, using the appropriate vehicle, and doing it frequently enough.

You generally target only people in a particular geographical area. If this is your target, then you won't be mailing, calling, or networking in a community far away from your area.

You might target individuals who meet certain criteria, or you might target a whole community. This implies a particular market strategy all driven by your clearly defined target. The more specific you can be with this definition, the better.

You might target first time home buyers or relocated families.

Who you define as your target is not important. What is important is that you define something. After all, you can't hit your target unless you know what you are aiming at.

Sentence four:
What marketing strategies, tactics, and weapons will you use to hit your target and ultimately achieve your marketing purpose?

This will be the longest part of your plan.

In this part of your plan, you identify all the marketing tactics you will employ. Make sure your list is practical and doable. You don't have to be fancy here, and don't overdo it. Plan what you realistically think you can do. Plan what you *realistically* think you can implement. Chances are it will be more than you are currently doing. Make some progress first before tackling more.

In the real estate business, the marketing tactics that have had the highest degree of success are the following:

A: Prospecting

B: Referral Strategies

C: Networking

D: Direct Sales

E: Direct Mail

F: PR

G: Telemarketing

Sure, other tactics work and produce results, but in studying some of the more successful real estate professionals, the list above represents the heart of a lot of the marketing done.

We will cover these ideas in more detail later in the book.

Sentence five:
What is your niche?

A niche is a tighter, usually smaller, segment of your target market. Once you identify your niche, you'll have no doubt where you are aiming.

Example niches for real estate agents include:

➢ The agent who specializes in golf course homes.

➢ The agent who lends his moving truck to new clients.

➢ The agent who concentrates on newly constructed homes.

Note: Beware of over-niching yourself. One real estate agent in Northern California is known as the "upper end home specialist." His tagline reads: "I only sell castles." Guess what? When the upper end market dries up, he sells NOTHING! So be versatile in your niche. When the upper end market is slow, this particular agent wishes he could sell mid to lower end properties, since they still bring in commission checks of over $10,000.

Sentence six:
What is your identity?

A lot of people would use the word "image" here. We don't, because usually image is something that isn't true, and we are big believers in integrity. That being said, we believe in telling clients and prospects who we really are, and so should you.

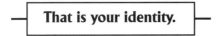

That is your identity.

To create your own identity, consider your answers to the following questions:

> ➤ What do you want clients to remember about you?
> ➤ How will they know you?
> ➤ Do you want to be known as a client friendly, professional, technically competent, service-oriented agent?
> ➤ Are you the responsive agent who meets every deadline and delivers your buying offers in a VW bug delivery vehicle?
> ➤ Are you the professional who drives around in the vehicle that looks like a house and passes out toy houses to all the kids?

Jerry has always lived by the phrase: "Make It Happen." Everyone knows him as the "Make It Happen" real estate agent. As a result, people want to work with him. Who wouldn't want to work with the Make It Happen guy? It's a great identity.

Go ahead and spell it out. What is unique about your look, how people remember you, and how you deliver your product? That's your identity.

Sentence seven:
How much money will you spend on your marketing?

A lot of people will try to peg a percentage of sales to this sentence. That's okay, because any plan is better than no plan.

A percentage, though, can be tricky, because so many businesses are in different stages of growth.

For example, a new real estate agent will spend more on marketing, theoretically, than an agent who has been in business a longer time. Likewise, an agent who has suffered a loss of major clients will spend more on marketing than an agent who has just received a few windfall listings.

If you must have a percentage, the average for small businesses is around four to five percent of revenue. If you want to be average, spend this amount. If you want to be above average spend more. However, limit expenses to less than twenty-five percent total.

Also, pay close attention to how you measure or allocate your marketing expenditures. It really doesn't matter how you measure it, just do it the same from year to year.

Now you have the seven sentences of a marketing plan. The more planning you do, the easier it will be to see if your marketing is working or what you need to adjust as you work through your plan. Don't take this step lightly.

We have shown you that planning doesn't have to be complex, but it has to be thought-out and deliberate.

Document your plan. Refer to it. Use it as a working document. Adjust when you have to.

Strategies to Kick Your Marketing Plan Up a Notch:

1)   Use an Excel spreadsheet to list your weapons and the month you will implement them.

2)   Ask your clients what they think your benefits are. You might be offering benefits you don't realize.

3)   Make a list of your competitors' benefits and make a list of yours. Find out what benefits they are offering that you aren't. Figure out how you can do the same or better.

4)   Set up a marketing mastermind planning group with clients or associates in similar industries (builders, mortgage companies, title companies, banks, etc.). Use this time as a give and take of ideas. You'll be amazed what great strategies and marketing techniques you can get from people in other fields.

5)   Always ask for business. If you don't ask the answer is always NO.

HIGH IMPACT STRATEGY NUMBER THREE: DEFINE YOUR COMPETITIVE ADVANTAGES

In the last section, we mentioned that the benefit you offer that your competition doesn't offer is your competitive advantage. We also mentioned that this is how you will accomplish your marketing purpose.

If you don't offer a benefit that your competition doesn't, then you need to analyze your strengths and core competencies.

Sometimes a competitive advantage is the result of a certain coverage set up that you have.

For example, maybe you have listing options that your competition doesn't. This presents a couple of scenarios.

> ➤ It allows you to offer a service that your competition doesn't.
> ➤ It allows you to offer a bundle of coverage at lower costs when your competitors are offering single offers.

A good example of this is referral incentives, home warranties, inspection allowances, etc. to enhance your service offering.

Sometimes your competitive advantage is related to certain knowledge or experience you possess that your competition doesn't.

For example, if you are an expert in a certain community and your clients come to you for that as well as ease of listing, that could be a competitive advantage.

If you are an agent for new home construction, and your competition struggles with that, you might have a competitive advantage by serving that niche.

Online listing information and communication is a nice benefit. If you are the only one doing business with a high degree of technology, you definitely have a competitive advantage, and you should market this aggressively.

Dig deep for your competitive advantage.

Maybe you are the only agent who has toys in your office or conference room for your clients' children to play with when meeting with prospective buyers.

Maybe you pay for all overnight delivery fees, separating you from the competition.

Maybe you pay for your clients' parking when they visit your office.

Don't overlook any aspect when determining your competitive advantages. Dig deep.

> **Once you define your competitive advantages, you are in a position to market them. Tell the world. Your competition can't.**

Advantages usually imply that you have something different than everyone else. This is important in the cluttered world of advertising.

If a client, reader, or browser spots something that they don't see anywhere else, then you will get noticed.

Imagine the bank that put in their ad the offer of free samples of their primary product. Imagine the hook of a free gift for the first ten respondents. Imagine the real estate agent who continually supplies comps and new listings for weekly price modification.

These are things you can bet the competition isn't offering; therefore, they are the things that increase your probability of being different, getting noticed, having an advantage, and eventually gaining a new client.

Strategies to Kick Your Competitive Advantages Up a Notch:

1) Make a list of all your benefits and all your competitions' benefits. What ones do you have that they don't?

2) Put your competitive advantages in all your promotional materials. You could say something like: "The ABC Real Estate Difference..." – then list all your competitive advantages.

3) Ask your clients, "If you could wave a magic wand and have one more benefit or advantage from me, what would it be?"

4) Write down your advantages. Use them in all your marketing—both online and off.

HIGH IMPACT STRATEGY NUMBER FOUR: IDENTIFY YOUR CORE SERVICES

In any study of marketing, products or services are a primary component. However, many people reserve this component for last, undeservingly so.

Simply state what you want to market (product/service) and to who (target), and you have more than half of your marketing done. Then you just need to figure out what and how to tell your target about your product/service.

─┤ **If only marketing were that easy!** ├─

We talk about the importance of core services more with real estate agents than we do with other types of businesses.

> **As a real estate agent, you have the ability to market certain types of homes that drive your product mix, which ultimately drive your profitability.**

Let's elaborate on this because it is very important.

If golf course homes are the most profitable part of your service mix, then you shouldn't have your largest percentage of marketing focused on first-time home buyers.

If listings offer you more margin than sales, then you should market accordingly.

> **We have seen bottom lines completely turn around with fewer sales simply by adjusting service mixes and focuses.**

41

Remember, direct sales is the major part of marketing that works for real estate agents. Once you decide what service mix you want, driven by your profitability goals, you can then develop your marketing messages for your direct selling efforts.

The same goes for your agency marketing. You want to advertise, publicize, and communicate all you can that's related to your service mix component and that your prospects most desire.

Apply this concept to all your marketing, even something as simple as your e-mail signature.

For example, your e-mail signature might look like one of these:

John Doe
Ask me today about FHA home loan qualification.

Or

Jane Doe
Free lifetime book-of-the-month club membership for all listings in the month of December.

Or

John Doe
Specializing in First Time Home Buyers

Or

Jane Doe
Commercial and Residential Real Estate in Montgomery County

These are just examples and thought starters. Please figure out what offer is best for you or what information will best drive your client/prospect to the mix component you want.

Understanding your core services and your product mix is an important part of marketing. You must know these elements so you know what marketing message to communicate to your target market and what action you want them to take. Always remember the purpose outlined in the first sentence of your marketing plan.

Strategies to Kick Your Core Services Up a Notch:

1)   Document your current service focus and mix.

2)   Calculate what profit increase you want and what a future product or service mix would look like.

3)   When evaluating a new service focus, assume a five percent change in mix towards the new item and see what impact it has on your profitability.

4)   Communicate to your clients very honestly about what your core service is and what you are an expert in. You don't necessarily need to say it's your highest margin product, but emphasize that you like to provide what you do best.

HIGH IMPACT STRATEGY NUMBER FIVE: DEFINE YOUR TARGET MARKETS

Think about how some businesses start out:

> They spend a lot of money identifying and communicating who they are to the marketplace.

> They build a brand.

> They lose it all when they add services unrelated to their core purpose and change who they really are.

Consider a long distance telephone company that starts selling phone hardware, or a gasoline station that begins serving fried chicken.

What about a real estate agent who, for example, adds more farm areas to work? Or a commercial broker who adds residential services?

Sometimes, shifts like these confuse clients, and they end up transferring their allegiance to an agent who better hits the target they are a part of. Clients always go where they feel the offer is more clearly defined and presented to *them*.

> **Targeting involves determining who buys what, why they buy it, where they buy it, and an assortment of similar questions. Identifying these factors is essential to marketing and using your resources efficiently.**

Think of it as narrowing your scope.

You have to know to whom you want to sell your products and services before you can successfully zero in on them with your marketing efforts. Clearly identifying your target will help you create marketing materials that hit your ideal prospects squarely on the bull's eye.

The real estate industry is getting more and more specialized, and carving out niches and marketing to those specialized niches is key.

Think about companies who supply only golf course community homes. The successful ones understand who they are, what their target market wants, how they buy and sell, and what keeps them happy.

Some agents have even defined their target market so narrowly that they specialize in simply selling town homes on golf courses to empty nesting parents.

Some agents provide specialized solutions for "difficult to find homes" segments. They specialize in listing and selling the unusual that appeal to that segment.

Before we go any further, realize that this does not mean that in order to succeed in targeting you need to change your business.

The important thing is to know what business you're in and what your typical clients want and need.

Then plan your sales and marketing messages and product offerings around those typical clients. That's target marketing.

We talk to a lot of independent real estate agents who ask, "How can I compete with larger brokers and agents?"

Our response is always the same:

"The best way to compete is to narrow your niche, then market and sell to that niche aggressively."

The secret to cultivating a niche is that the more time you spend in it, the more of an expert you become, and the more you expand your territory.

So when it comes to targeting, plan ahead. Start by asking, "Who will benefit most from my products and services?"

Begin building a detailed profile of your current clients. To do so, answer the following questions:

➢ Why do they do business with you?

➢ What do they have in common?

➢ How can you best service their current and future needs?

Then, think about the "perfect client." If you could magically create the "ideal client," what would he or she look like?

You can break down your target in several ways:

Geographically

➢ Where are your current clients?

➢ What is the size and density of the area you serve?

➢ How far out can you realistically stretch your market without stretching your resources?

Demographically

➢ Who is the typical client you sell to or who lists with you?

➢ Are they blue collar or white collar workers?

➢ Do they have children?

➢ What size house do they buy?

Products/Services

➢ What do you sell most often: Repeat buyers, relocating home buyers, first time home buyers, etc.?

Strategies to Kick Your Target Markets Up a Notch:

1)   Analyze what markets your top twenty-five clients are in. Are there any patterns? Can you find more clients in these target markets?

2)   Are there target markets you want to target but are not doing business in now? What do they want and how can you develop business in those target markets?

3)   Are there target markets you are doing business in that don't fit you as well? Would it be worth not doing business with this target market?

4)   Define your ideal client. What implications does this have for who you target?

HIGH IMPACT STRATEGY NUMBER SIX: FIGURE OUT A CLIENT'S LIFETIME VALUE

Recently, Al's company spent $600 on a postcard mailing to a list of about 1,500 names. Now, we know it takes more than one contact to a prospect to get that person to take action. In this case, however, a prospect responded to the mailing and placed an enrollment for a three employee group order that totaled about $600 in commissions. One of Al's employees stated that they broke even on the mailing.

At that, Al immediately spoke up with passion and said, "No, we did way better than that."

The unassuming employee asked why it was better than breaking even.

The answer is simple. That client Al's company satisfied for $600 on an initial placement will be back. That client will return for more services in the future, over and over, as long as they are satisfied.

If that client buys more over the next ten years, then that client is worth more in gross sales. Over a lifetime, the total could be significant, especially as they order other services and products. You can now start to see what the true value of a client is over the lifetime of their purchasing.

Why is this important?

Because at some point you will be making decisions on how much to invest in clients. Investments could be in the form of free offers, your time, etc. You would make different decisions based on the initial $600 order versus a lifetime of value of over $20,000.

The same goes for an initial listing and sale for a client versus three or four listings and sales during the lifetime of that same client.

Think of this concept related to all clients. You need this information to see which clients are worth focusing attention on and to identify which of your clients will never justify the expense it takes to keep them fully satisfied.

The lifetime value of a client goes even beyond this simple example. What if this same client referred one or two or more clients just like them to you? Without this client you wouldn't have received that referral. What is the lifetime value of that client now? That value just took an exponential leap.

This is called marketing geometrically versus linearly.

Strategies to Kick Your Lifetime Value Up a Notch:

1)   Don Peppers and Martha Rodgers have a nice lifetime value calculator available at this website: **http://www.marketingbasecamp.com/html/life_ time_value.html**.

2)   You don't have to actually figure to the penny the lifetime value. You just need a relative number to justify your time and expense for a particular client.

3)   Pick an unsuspecting client and tell him or her about this concept. Use this client as an example of the lifetime value of a client. It might be a good selling tool.

HIGH IMPACT STRATEGY NUMBER SEVEN: START NETWORKING

W e've all heard that networking should be an integral part of our total marketing plan, but what exactly is networking? Is it the same for offline marketing as it is for online marketing?

Simply stated, networking is any contact to establish relationships that can lead to business. Sometimes the path to business is direct, such as meeting someone face-to-face to discuss business; other times it is indirect, such as through referrals.

Everyone you know knows someone else who needs your products or services. This is the most important rule of networking.

Many people go to a networking event hoping to do business—to close a deal.

It simply doesn't work that way.

Your goal of attending a networking event is to meet two or three people, find a reason to follow up with them, and then start a relationship. The business will most likely come later, from an indirect referral of someone they know who needs your products or services.

Networking means making these contacts and building on them by talking with people about what you do and who you are. It also involves listening to them to uncover how you might assist them in what they do.

These contacts, the people you need to know or the people who can help you, might be right under your nose. To help build that list, answer the following:

➢ Who has taken an interest in you lately or in the past?

➢ Who have you been good friends with?

➢ Who do you always talk business with when you get together?

➢ Who has helped you or offered encouragement or advice in your business?

This list could go on and on, but the general notion is that we are already networking. Networking is all around us, and the people to build our network with are with us every day.

The other thing you can do is fill in the name of a person next to a particular classification, like "friend," "neighbor," "former employer," etc. A good example of this is when Al learned how valuable the parents of his daughter's sports teammates were in his network. Standing on the sidelines of soccer game, Al had conversations with the other parents that included the following questions: "What do you do?" "Where do you work?" "Do you know anyone who…?" And the rest, as they say, is history.

For more on How to Instantly Add 50 People to Your Network visit,
www.networkingworkbook.com **or**
www.market-for-profits.com/set_revenue_cds.html
for the Networking Power Pack.

Networking is not only important from a business standpoint, but also from a resource standpoint. Do you ever need those hard-to-get tickets for that important family member coming to town? Do you ever need that recipe from the family reunion you just went to? Need a tip on parenting a certain situation? You can obtain all these things from your networking groups. Your networking groups serve as resources for not only business related things, but also for just about anything you can think of.

Networking just doesn't happen. It has to be part of your marketing plan with activity and initiatives associated with it, an established time table, and responsibility assigned. Networking is a learned skill. Few people are born with the required networking skills. You must learn the skills because they are part of a total process, not a one time event (as is often said about all of marketing).

The key components of the networking process are:

➢ Planning which networking events to attend.

➢ Setting networking goals in total and for each event.

➢ Knowing who to target in the process of networking.

➢ Building relationships.

➢ Establishing trust as well as showing interest.

➢ Following up.

➢ Continuing the relationship.

Here's a great example of a networking event.

Every year Jerry hosts a client appreciation party called "The Cuban Carnival." It started with 200 attendees and now it attracts up to 1,200. Jerry tracks and updates the guest list at the door and adds any new people to his database. On the sheet the attendees fill in at the entrance, they sign whether or not Jerry can call them for real estate related information. No one minds, because they are at a party and having fun. Most of the parties end up being done for free, since his affiliates (lenders, title and escrow, home warranty companies) help with most of the event expenses. However, even if the event costs something, it is well justified by the referral business he receives from it. Talk about networking efficiency! At an event like this you are the center of attention and what all the guests are talking about.

Strategies to Kick Your Networking Up a Notch:

Following are thirty-five groups, associations, or clubs that might include you in their networking. The next time you want something or need a resource, try one of these groups. If you don't have a group, start one.

1) Alumni Clubs

2) Neighborhood Associations

3) Block Party Committee

4) Parent Teacher Organizations

5) Church Committees

6) Chambers of Commerce

7) Board of Director Groups

8) Online Forum Groups

9) Collector Clubs

10) Book Group at Local Book Store

11) Sports Coaching Group

12) Boy Scouts/Girl Scouts

13) Talent Show/Musical

14) Parade/Event Committee

15) Investment Clubs

16) Private Online Forum Group

17) Public Online Forum Group

18) Barber Shop Regulars

19) Restaurant Regulars

20) Non Profit Volunteer

21) Political Campaign

22) School Room Mom/Dad

23) Sports League, especially golf and bowling

24) Craft Group (quilting bee)

25) Adult Education Class

26) Professional Associations

27) Day Care Moms Group

28) Ladies Night Out

29) Men's Poker Night

30) Business Before Hours Groups (e.g. at trains stations)

31) Business After Hours Groups

32) Business Roundtables

33) Seminar Reunions

34) Class Reunions

35) Family Reunions

See how well you do in each part of the networking process. Grade yourself. What does it take to improve in those areas where you scored low?

High Impact Strategy
Number Eight:
Develop a Referral Strategy

We often hear that in business, it's not *what* you know that counts; it's *who* you know…or better yet, *who knows you.* In the last chapter, we reviewed how business networking should be part of everyone's marketing plan. Associated with networking is the whole subject of referrals.

While a referral strategy is different than a networking strategy, there are some gray areas.

In a nutshell, the difference between referral programs and networking is that networking is any contact to establish relationships that lead to business, and referrals are an indirect subset of networking: knowing someone who knows someone who could use your products or services.

Yes, it can be somewhat of a gray area, but they both involve knowing a group of people.

Real estate agents often ask: "What is the best way to get referrals?" or more specifically "What exactly do you say? Is there a preferred phraseology to use when getting referrals?"

The best way to obtain referrals is to directly ask clients for them. Nothing special. Nothing fancy. People like to give referrals because they like to help others. A referral is a way of helping people.

A suggested phraseology would be something along the lines of "narrowing your universe."

Instead of asking who do you know who could use your products or services, ask the question about a smaller group. For example, "Jim, who do you know at your Chamber of Commerce meetings who is thinking of buying or selling a home?"

You just narrowed Jim's universe, and he is more likely to think of someone versus asking him to exhaust his total network to think of someone.

The best time to ask for referrals is at the height of client satisfaction.

If a client compliments you, ask for a referral.

If a client starts raving about your service or product, ask for a referral.

When clients are in a positive frame of mind they gladly give you the name of someone they want to have the same positive experience.

Clients are loyal and like to give referrals. Think how good you feel when you are able to find baseball tickets for a requesting friend or client. The same thing applies to referrals. When you are able to help someone out with a referral, the other person thinks more of you, and you are proud to have helped.

From a marketing standpoint, anything you can do to condition yourself or put a system in place to automatically request referrals will increase your referral success. Maybe you can set a goal to ask five past clients a week for referrals via e-mail or a letter. Maybe you automatically ask every new client you encounter for someone they know who would enjoy the same set of benefits they enjoy from you.

There is nothing fancy about referrals and referral programs. It boils down to always asking for referrals directly. Your referral program can be very simple and can be a great leverage point for geometrically growing your business.

All real estate agents need to make more of an effort to get referral business from current clients, since these are the individuals who currently spend one hundred percent of their time talking and thinking about real estate. If you are doing a great job for your current clients, then they will refer you to others.

Strategies to Kick Your Referrals Up a Notch:

1) Send a restaurant gift card to anyone whose referral does business with you.

2) Define your ideal client and let all your clients know what that looks like in case they run into someone fitting your definition.

3) Offer to help a client with their referral program.

4) Ask others what referral programs work that they have used.

5) Make it your goal that for every transaction you do, you will get at least one or two referrals from that client. Imagine what would happen to your business if you only focused on this one thing and made it happen. You would at least double your business with this one activity.

HIGH IMPACT STRATEGY NUMBER NINE: BE CONSISTENT WITH YOUR COMMISSIONS STRUCTURE

> **Michael Porter, an American educator said it best,
> "Cutting prices is usually insanity if the
> competition can go as low as you can."**

You've also probably heard the phrase, "Live by price; die by price."

Both of these statements are very true. Therefore, you must ingrain both of them into your memory.

Does that mean you should never reduce your commissions? Well, there are two schools of thought on this. Al believes there is a right time to use price as a marketing weapon and a wrong time.

Here's the reasoning behind Al's position on this topic: You don't want to be known as a discounter or the lowest priced agent in the business. Additionally, if you give something you should get something in return. However, using price to drive higher volumes adds to your profitability, because you truly do incur the economies of scale.

So, as Al teaches, if you are not completely booked during the prime buying and selling season for your market, using price product mix to obtain volume can be okay. Still, in this case, get something if you give something. Maybe the thing you get is three solid listing referrals.

On the other hand, Jerry has a totally different viewpoint on this topic. He is a firm believer that in order to build a great real estate business, you need to be consistent with your commission pricing. If you start to discount your fee for the aggressive negotiating prospect,

61

and you charge a full fee to the sweet little old couple, you're the one who'll get burned. When the sweet little old couple finds out that you lowered your fee for someone else, they may not be so sweet to you anymore.

Therefore, you must have a standard and stick to it. Jerry's experience has taught him that a lot of times, the clients who haggle the most over price are going to be so time consuming that you can probably close two transactions in the time it takes you to close theirs.

So who is right? Al or Jerry? Only you can decide that and do what's best for your real estate business. Now you have both sides of the story and can make the best decision for your circumstances.

Strategies to Kick Your Pricing Up a Notch:

1) Print out an offering sheet that packages many services together (such as lender and warranty information) to get the highest price for your primary service.

2) Offer great incentives for any of your own listings being sold without another real estate agent involved.

3) Justify your commission by stressing the value you offer. When clients truly understand all that you do, they'll never ask for a commission reduction again.

4) Develop your confidence. Your ability to present yourself confidently creates value to the client. It shows that you're the right person to get the job done, no matter what the cost.

HIGH IMPACT STRATEGY
NUMBER TEN:
OFFER A GUARANTEE

"One hundred percent unconditionally guaranteed!" Sounds pretty good, doesn't it. Chances are, when you first said it as a business owner, that phrase scared you to death. But when your clients first heard it, they were at ease, had confidence in your work, and trusted you to the point of doing business.

> **The number one reason people do business with you is because they trust you. Your level of confidence is number two.**

Trust and confidence go a long way in doing business, whether it is the first transaction or one of many.

People will always view working with someone they don't know as a risk. It's human nature to be skeptical of strangers. Therefore, anything you can do to reduce or even remove that risk increases the probability of prospects doing business with you.

A guarantee of any sort reduces that risk.

Don't fake it. Offer a real guarantee, no questions asked. If you start putting a bunch of fine print and conditions with your guarantee, you lose the effect quickly. Clients are smarter than you think about guarantees.

A guarantee can also be a competitive advantage. What are your competitors guaranteeing?

As a real estate agent, you likely guarantee your service anyway, so why not blow your horn about it? If you supply a contract to a client, and they have a complaint, you offer to take care of it to salvage the deal and to retain the other party's trust and confidence. How is this different from a guarantee? Make a big deal about it. Promote it. You will reap more in return than your risk of a guarantee being exercised.

Strategies to Kick Your Guarantees Up a Notch:

1) Print up labels that read "100% Guaranteed!" and place them on proposals, brochures, marketing materials, etc.

2) Keep track of business you think you received because you offered a guarantee and measure them against the amount of guarantees that were exercised.

3) State that each part of the buying and selling process is guaranteed: the listing, the no-pressure approach, the offer, the contract delivery, buying satisfaction, etc. It's okay to be imaginative.

High Impact Strategy Number Eleven: Do Some Online Marketing

These days it's hard to find anyone in the workplace who remembers doing business without a fax machine. In its day, the fax machine was cutting edge technology, and it quickly became a staple of any and all businesses, regardless of size or type. The same thing is happening today with web sites, e-mail, and anything Internet related.

More and more real estate transactions are happening in the digital world. This requires movement of files electronically from client to agent, and sometimes back. It also involves viewing listings, making offers, and communicating online.

Yes, the Internet is here to stay and is a competitive mainstay more than an advantage. Those who have responded to this change will remain in business and may even thrive. Those who don't will join the scrap pile that includes wax fax paper and typewriters.

We could write an entire book about online marketing, so for now we will just scratch the surface of online marketing and review a few of the fundamentals as they relate to your real estate business.

> **Defining your objectives and having a plan is as important for online marketing as it is for all other marketing.**

Here are some things to consider: You want a web site, but what are you going to do with it? You have e-mail, but do you communicate effectively with it and to the right people?

These are the types of things you want in your plan and the types of questions you want to answer in order to go forward towards success. Online marketing is not a panacea. Online marketing is more than a web site and e-mail.

> **Choosing what is right for your business, the marketing of your products and services, and what your target market likes, wants, and needs will determine your online course of action.**

Web Site

A web site is an address. It is your house on the Internet. First you want people to find your house. Then you want them to feel welcomed and comfortable enough to stay and chat, or at least interact with you. You want to get to know each other to the point of wanting to know more about each other. Once this happens, you want to get to the point of trust so that you can partner together in the buying and selling of real estate. A web site can do all this.

A web site can collect prospect names for this relationship exercise. This kind of interaction is much more effective and personal than a brochure.

A web site is a tool to interact with a prospect and/or a client. You want to supply enough information and value so that prospects leave their name (for you to follow up with later) or for them to return for another visit. Ultimately, getting them to list with you or hire you as their buyer's agent is your goal.

You must integrate your online marketing efforts with all other marketing activity. Your web site should be connected with your company's offline, more traditional marketing efforts.

> **You can successfully drive traffic to a web site with a combination of online and traditional offline marketing.**

E-mail

Sending and receiving e-mail is the most popular use of the Internet. Just look at your own e-mail activity. If you're like most people, your e-mail usage has exploded. Unfortunately, e-mail usage in general has also exploded in abuse. We highly suggest and recommend that you operate within ethical parameters in all marketing, especially e-mail.

First, do not send spam messages. Do not send messages to people who have not given you permission to market to them. Do not buy or rent e-mail lists to send to. Let common sense and permission-based activity prevail.

For most real estate agents, permission-based e-mail marketing campaigns are the most memorable and cost-effective way to reach new and existing clients. This can consist of e-mail newsletters or targeted personalized e-mail messages.

E-mail marketing can be a tool for branding, direct response, and building client relationships. It's cheap, easy to use, and almost everybody surfing the Internet has an e-mail address.

> **E-mail marketing includes every e-mail you send to a client or prospect, such as direct promotional e-mails to interested prospects and informational e-mails sent to acquire new clients or sell to existing clients. You can also use e-mail marketing to keep in touch with clients, to encourage client loyalty, and to further client relationships.**

To be an e-mail marketer, you can send a direct e-mail message, an electronic newsletter (e-zine), or an online advertisement. One difference between this type of marketing and the print equivalent is that you must only send electronic mail when you have permission. Another difference is that e-mail can be interactive, with links to home photos, for example.

Sending e-mail is very cost effective and many times free. E-mail is also very targeted. When you have a good hook, your response rate can be higher than regular mail. The important thing is to keep your promises and play by the rules. Doing so will make you a marketing winner through and through.

Auto-responders

One goal of marketing is to do it consistently and automatically, if possible. Auto-responders accomplish both. Auto-responders are programs set up to automatically respond via e-mail when triggered. Most auto-responders are triggered by a blank e-mail sent to the auto-responder e-mail address (e.g. "for information on guerrilla marketing coaching send a blank e-mail to **gmcoach@market-for-profits.com**.")

When someone sends an e-mail to that auto-responder address, the sender receives an already prepared e-mail message with the requested information. This happens automatically and almost instantaneously depending on some Internet and e-mail servers.

For your real estate business, you may want to use an auto-responder for people who inquire about your real estate services. The message can be a standard overview of what you offer and why you're the best agent for the job. This will save you lots of time replying to e-mail messages from people who simply want to know more about you.

An E-zine

An e-zine is an on-line newsletter. Publishing your own free e-zine can bring huge amounts of qualified traffic to your web site while helping you to increase your profits. Today, more and more people publish their own e-zine. You have likely seen them all over the Internet, and you probably subscribe to a few.

E-zines are a great mechanism to keep in touch with clients and prospects. As you know by now, constant client and prospect contact is vital to your marketing success. Did you know that it takes six to eight "touches" to convert a prospect to a client? E-zines can be one more touch in an efficient and effective marketing world.

Not only will an e-zine allow you to maintain regular contact with your web site visitors, but it will also act as a reminder to them to revisit your site.

Online PR

One of the most cost-effective ways to publicize and market your business is to use the many PR tools, methods, and opportunities that exist online. Many of these are simple and either free or low-cost PR options.

With online PR, you're simply taking traditional PR (discussed in High Impact Strategy Number Sixteen) and extending it to the online community. This includes targeting online and traditional media that have a significant online presence and sending them your press release (see High Impact Strategy Number Sixteen for press release writing guidelines).

In addition to promoting interaction with individuals, online PR allows for a very wide distribution of news and information.

You can successfully drive traffic to your web site when you use a combination of online and traditional offline marketing. Using the tools we just discussed will put you further ahead than your competition and closer to your prospect's and client's wallets.

Strategies to Kick Your Online Marketing Up a Notch:

1)   Some of the more popular and user-friendly press release distribution sites are **www.prweb.com**, **www.pressbox.com**, and **www.webwire.com**.

2)   Items and information to offer in an auto-responder message include:

   ➤ A free report about the current real estate market

   ➤ A checklist of items to consider before listing your property

   ➤ A top ten list of why now is the perfect time to buy real estate

   ➤ An article you authored to showcase your expertise

   ➤ A free book chapter you authored

   ➤ A community guide to interested home buyers

   ➤ A booklet of real estate facts

   ➤ An e-book about home buying or selling strategies

   ➤ A mortgage calculator worksheet

3)   Recommended auto responder program: **www.aweber.com/?201116**

4)   Your e-mail signature should always include your name, contact information, and web site. This can drive interested prospects to your web site. Be sure to read and be in compliance with the current CAN-SPAM laws.

HIGH IMPACT STRATEGY NUMBER TWELVE: INVEST IN ADVERTISING

When Al tells people that he is a marketing coach and consultant, he sometimes gets the response, "Oh, so you help people with their advertising."

This response may be correct sometimes, but it is not true all the time. Because Al is such an advocate of low and no cost marketing, he often saves advertising for last.

However, some people still insist on advertising first. Advertising has both pros and cons.

Advertising sends your message to the masses. By that definition, you may be sending your message to people who don't care about you, aren't interested in buying or selling real estate, and are not ideal prospects for you. In other words, advertising in this situation totally misses the target.

In other cases, people in your target market will see your message. When this happens, advertising did hit the target.

But honestly, why take the chance when you can do so much more marketing that will hit the target.

> **Advertising works when it hits the target, is done consistently, and stands out from all other advertising.**

That is a tall order for this marketing weapon.

Consistent advertising implies a larger than average expenditure or budget. Advertising that stands out means you better be darn creative or have the means (again, more money) to hire an agency.

However, some advertising does stand out and is not agency generated.

> **Any "hook" you can include in your ad that causes the prospect to react or respond to you is advertising that stands out from the pack.**

We will talk about hooks later, but many times a hook is nothing more than free information, free samples, free consultations, etc.

If you are going to attempt to create your own ad, keep in mind the marketing formula: AIDA

AIDA stands for Attention, Interest, Desire, and Action.

You have to get the reader or viewer's attention. You do this either with an eye-catching graphic and/or a very creative, large bold headline. That's the way the eye follows an ad: graphics first, headlines second.

Next, you have to get the prospects' interest and create the desire through easy-to-read information. You can do this through bulleted points of information, captions, quotes, or anything other than straight, plain, boring text. These are the things the eye will follow after the graphics and the headline.

Finally, include a call to action. People like help making decisions. They don't mind being told what to do. Some good calls to action include "Call today," "Visit our web site," and "Send in for free information." Put some sort of call to action in all your advertising, direct mail, and e-mail marketing efforts.

One advertising technique we have seen work in the real estate business is using the designation in your classified and display ads as "Home of the Month."

Any designation that separates you from your competition will gain readers' attention and stand out from other advertising.

Strategies to Kick Your Advertising Up a Notch:

1) Plan your advertising. Ask:

   ➢ What is the purpose of the ad?

   ➢ Who is it targeted to?

   ➢ What is my message?

   ➢ What is my call to action?

   ➢ What kind of response do I need to justify the expense?

   ➢ Did it work?

   ➢ What is the frequency the ad will run?

2) Buy the book *Guerrilla Advertising*.

3) Read a magazine or newspaper real fast. See what ads get your attention.

4) Read an ad and try not to pay attention to the visuals. Did it communicate a message that would entice you to take action?

HIGH IMPACT STRATEGY NUMBER THIRTEEN: SEND DIRECT MAIL PIECES

How much "junk mail" did you get today? Hopefully none.

In the printing business they call it "love mail" because they love to print it.

Now you probably received some love mail that others call junk mail.

> **Mail that arrives to a non-intended target is junk (love). Mail that hits the target is good mail and effective marketing.**

Now you have key number one: Make sure you have the right target defined for your direct mail. Here's key number two: Make sure your direct mail hits the target you define. Notice the two parts here. They are different.

Once you have a target defined and are aiming at it, make sure you are using the right vehicle to carry your message. This could be a postcard, letter, third class mail, brochure, or some other vehicle.

For visibility and quick communication of your message with a call to action, postcards work best. Postcards don't need an envelope, and there is a high probability that the recipient will read both sides before putting it aside or throwing it away.

Some letters end up in the trash unopened because the receiver identified them as direct mail that was of no interest.

After deciding which vehicle to use, you must make sure your message is right. Are you communicating benefits, pain questions, information, teasers, etc?

We have found that the optimum design for postcards is an attention getting graphic, headline, or question on the front (and nothing else so as to cause the receiver to turn it over). On the back include three or four benefit statements or pain questions, a hook, and contact information. Don't forget to leave space for a return address, a stamp, and addressing.

The hook is most important. A good hook will increase your response from a few tenths of a percent to over five percent in some cases.

Now that you have determined the target, vehicle, and message, all that's left is to determine the frequency.

Once a month is optimum. Once every three weeks is aggressive. Once a week is an annoyance. Once a quarter is effective but slower.

Have a plan. Plan at least six months worth of mailings. If you are going to mail just once, save your money. You are only betting on luck if you do. Touch your prospects with your mailing as often as you can without being an annoyance.

Don't forget to calculate the postage cost in your overall direct mail budget/expenditures.

Design a good direct mail piece and hit the same target often and you will increase your business.

When Jerry started his postcard campaign, he was committed to the program for a one year period. He says that the first few months felt like a total waste of money. However, when he started offering something of value, like a NO COST property market evaluation that looked like a coupon, the calls started to come in. In fact, the postcard mailing was so effective that today he invests about $60,000 annually in postcard mailings. Now, you might think that seems crazy. But it's not crazy when that one form of marketing brings in an additional $250,000 per year to your bottom line. The key is to spend it when you have it and not before.

For more on postcard marketing for real estate marketing, contact The Ink Well at 1-800-inkwell or **www.1-800-inkwell.com**.

Strategies to Kick Your Direct Mail Up a Notch:

1) If you have a list of 4,000 and can afford to mail to it once, take the best 1,000 names and mail four times to just those 1,000. Yes, this means ignoring the other 3,000 names, but you will have a higher response.

2) Use odd shapes for your postcards, but get post office approval.

3) Use colored envelopes to attract attention and stand out.

4) Make direct mail look like an urgent overnight package. It will arrive at your target's desk and get opened.

5) Put yourself on your own mailing list to track the post office timing and condition the mail arrives in.

6) Combine your list with a power partner's list. Get twice the reach at half the cost.

High Impact Strategy Number Fourteen: Write Sales Letters

After reading this strategy title, you're likely thinking: "You're so gung-ho on postcards. I'm surprised to even see this chapter in the book."

The fact is, sales letters still work, especially when you have a situation where you must communicate more information than will fit on a postcard.

Letters can be more personal and less mass produced. Letters can include instructions, ideas, requests, and other information. Letters can be folded around and accompany a business card, an article of interest, or some other item that adds value to the prospect.

If you are using sales letters as "touches" in your marketing campaign, you need to plan them out, just as you do a postcard mailing.

Handwritten letters will really get attention. You can even run these on a printing press to look like they were handwritten. People might figure this out, but the letter still will stand out versus the "boilerplate" letters.

Personalize your sales letters. Write Dear Mr. Smith, not Dear Friend or Dear Client. Take advantage of the opportunity to mail merge your letters. With today's desktop technology and inexpensive laser printing, you can easily mail merge your letters. Your word processing program will likely have a tutorial of how to do so.

If you have larger quantities than you can handle in-house, outsource the mailing to a mail house or letter shop.

Sales letters are good to intermingle with postcards during a campaign or series of mailings. Do a sales letter the first, third, and fifth week, and a postcard the second, fourth, and sixth week.

Always hold your letter content to one page, and most of all, use a Postscript.

> **Many statistics cite how often prospects act on a P.S. or how a P.S. can increase the letter's response rate.**

Letter marketing doesn't have to be fancy. Just write from your heart and give some valuable information so you can stay in front of your prospects.

Strategies to Kick Your Sales Letters Up a Notch:

1) Write the letter fast; it will simulate speaking and take the worry out of crafting the letter.

2) Use bullets of information.

3) Use a headline. Reading a letter is much like reading an ad. People look for graphics, headlines, bullets, and then text. The only difference is sometimes the P.S. is read first.

4) Use the direct mail principles discussed earlier:

   ➢ Target

   ➢ Message

   ➢ Vehicle (this will be the letter)

   ➢ Frequency

5) Make your letter mailing three dimensional. This means putting something lumpy in your mailing like candy, mints, trinkets, etc.

HIGH IMPACT STRATEGY NUMBER FIFTEEN: CREATE BROCHURES

A re you in the real estate business, or the business of providing happy homes for clients? Consider this when designing your brochures.

> **When a client states that he or she wants your real estate services, the person is really saying, "I want hassle free options to consider and hassle free buying procedures so I can start living in my new home and enjoy it."**

This is your chance to be an expert and help them make the decision that meets their requirements.

Put the information from this book with that philosophy and you are now a home ownership consultant for your client. Go back to the niche chapter, highlight the skills that qualify you for this niche, and place that in your brochure.

Remember, sell the benefits, not the features.

Talk about insurance considerations and various financing options you know about, and then use the AIDA principles (Attention, Interest, Desire, and Action) to get down to the way people make home buying and selling decisions.

Just these things alone make you a real estate expert in your clients' eyes. You are already doing it. Now blow your horn about it.

Brochures are often tri-fold in design, but not always. They can be one, two, or four color. You can use them to present information, showcase your listings, and as a "leave behind" on a listing presentation.

Never pass out your brochures to unsuspecting and uninterested suspects. Make sure you have a high probability of interest before giving away a brochure. Sure, you may at times leave a stack of brochures in a rack, such as at your local Chamber of Commerce, but that's the exception, not the norm.

Treat the design of your brochure much like the design of a sales call. Introduce yourself; understand the client's pain, challenges and needs; demonstrate the solutions you offer; relate information about how others have used your services successfully; and then tell them or ask them to take action. That's all there is to a brochure. Sounds easy, doesn't it? Well, it's not always that easy, but you should always put this kind of thought behind it.

> **Don't think people will read every word of your brochure. That's why you must make sure your benefits stand out.**

Make good use of headlines, sub-headlines, bullets, captions, and quotes.

A brochure can act as your sales force absentia, but don't just drop it and run.

Follow up, touch the prospect with more marketing, and always be closing.

Strategies to Kick Your Brochures Up a Notch:

1) Testimonials in your brochure give you credibility and help your prospects relate to you. Contact us if you need one.

2) Use a brochure as a hook or fulfillment for a request from your other marketing.

3) Don't try to tell your whole story with a brochure. If it is too much information, consider a series of brochures.

4) Make an offer to help your client with the design and implementation of their financing and affordability options or even design options if you are in the new construction real estate business.

5) Include a brochure in the paperwork delivered to your new client.

High Impact Strategy Number Sixteen: Do Some PR

Public relations (PR) is a favorite among marketers. Here you will learn how to get your name in the media at no cost. Do it more than once and clients and prospects will say to you, "I see your name everywhere."

That is the goal with PR; it is just another touch, but the price is right.

If you do PR correctly, you will establish incredible credibility, a huge following, and word of mouth exposure more than you have now.

Here's how it starts: Write a simple press release. Yes, we know you are not a writer, you don't know what goes in a press release, and you can't think what to write a press release about or who to send it to. That's okay. We'll fix that right now and quickly.

Writing a press release is simpler than you imagine.

A press release must be about some newsworthy event. The first paragraph should cover the five Ws – who, what, where, when, why – and how. Don't beat around the bush here. Get right to the point. We have seen printed news blurbs that are only the first paragraph of a press release. Editors don't like to waste time any more than you do. Respect the five Ws and how.

Make sure you have a quote from *you* in the press release. Didn't know you could be quoted? Sure you can. "Just put down what you would say and put quotation marks around it," stated Al Lautenslager, co-author of this book.

Close with contact information, brief bio information, and your web site or e-mail address.

That's it.

> **Over sixty percent of the information in a
> newspaper comes from a press release.**

Now about those topics. What do you write a press release about?

Every year you have an anniversary. That's news and worthy of a press release.

Anytime you move, introduce new products and services, hire someone new or promote someone, you can write a press release.

Doing a good deed with a non-profit organization, joining a board of directors, reaching a milestone, and teaming up with someone in a joint venture are all ideas for a newsworthy press release.

VERY IMPORTANT:

— Keep it newsworthy; editors hate promotion. —

Send the press release to editors via e-mail or fax. You can send it snail mail, but that takes too long sometimes and is almost old fashioned.

Do not call to follow up on a press release.

Don't ask editors if they received the press release or if they will publish it. Either of these questions will guarantee that the release **WILL NOT** be published.

Send your release to news reporters, feature editors, magazine editors, and producers of your local radio and TV shows.

We told you it was simple. Plan it out and issue a press release about something every other month and you will soon hear that prospects and clients see you "everywhere."

<u>Strategies to Kick Your PR Up a Notch:</u>

1)   Have a goal to write nine press releases in eighteen months.

2)   If news comes up, write a press release. Don't worry about your schedule and plan. News is news when it happens.

3)   Use press releases as direct mail pieces; post them on your web site and use them as handouts with clients and prospects.

4)   Make sure your clients know about your news before it hits the media.

5)   Post your press releases online for free at **www.prweb.com.**

HIGH IMPACT STRATEGY NUMBER SEVENTEEN: DEVELOP YOUR EXPERT STATUS

M any times we will recommend to people just starting out in real estate or even just starting out in marketing to position themselves as an expert.

You are an expert in something. If you have your name on a For Sale sign or are advertising yourself as a real estate professional, you better be professing yourself to be an expert in some facet of your business.

Maybe you are a financing expert, a new home construction expert, a community expert, or all of the above.

Once you say you are an expert, you are an expert. Don't be shy about this. Your clients will respect and trust you even more, because people like to buy from experts.

If you are not sure about your expert status, study up. Learn all you can about a certain segment of your profession or your market. Find other experts in an area and see what they know.

Whatever you do, position yourself as an expert of some type.

Becoming an Expert

How do you position yourself as the expert besides saying that you are?

> ➢ Write an article.
> ➢ Do a radio interview.
> ➢ Write a press release.

➢ Write a column for a newsletter or newspaper.

➢ Speak to an audience of any kind.

➢ Create your own newsletter or e-zine.

➢ Write for your own web site or someone else's.

All of these strategies clearly tell your audience that you know what you are talking about enough to share the information with others. That makes you an expert.

Strategies to Kick Your Expert Status Up a Notch:

1) Have someone interview you over the phone, record it, and have the recording as a giveaway, a product to sell, or another piece of credibility to make you an expert.

2) Make an attempt at writing your bio as it would appear at the end of a magazine article.

3) Call the local Rotary Club or Chamber of Commerce to see if you can speak to a group of their members on the latest trends in your area of expertise.

4) Develop a list of speaking and writing topics that you could offer as an expert.

HIGH IMPACT STRATEGY NUMBER EIGHTEEN: SEND THANK YOU NOTES

When Al visited a client's office the other day, he saw that she had one of his handwritten thank you notes hanging on her personal bulletin board. He asked why it was hanging there. The client replied that no one had ever sent her a handwritten thank you note before.

At that moment Al knew that if he can be set apart from the competition just by taking five minutes to handwrite a thank you note, he would do it for many other clients.

Jerry, too, is fanatic about writing thank you notes. He writes at least five per day, every day. You should, too.

People appreciate the time, the thought, and the touch of a handwritten thank you note. Many people won't believe that we have this as a marketing strategy, but all we ask is that you try it. You will not believe the results.

First, people will open a handwritten envelope almost all the time. And if they open the envelope, they will definitely read the enclosed handwritten note.

Thank people for their time. Thank people for doing business with you. Acknowledge special occasions like birthdays, graduations, promotions, milestones reached, and any other successes you hear about.

We like to sign the note with our initials or name, and then we put a famous quote underneath related to success, opportunity, partnership, teamwork, or some other motivational topic. This adds a nice touch.

Make sure your message is sincere. Don't make it sound like a mass mailing message that you are writing on everyone else's thank you note.

Cite something of interest or some uniqueness you know about your client or prospect.

Don't worry about sounding emotional. We call it professional emotion. Professional emotion bonds professional relationships, which maintains loyalty and eventually increases business.

Strategies to Kick Your Thank You Notes Up a Notch:

1)   Use a fountain pen. This adds a touch of class to your personalization.

2)   Only use black ink.

3)   It's okay to include your business card inside the note.

4)   Include an article of interest or a clipping of your client's name in the paper.

5)   Don't limit your thank you gestures to just notes. A nice gift basket, a dinner gift certificate, or tickets to an event also set you apart from your competition in the world of thank you notes.

High Impact Strategy Number Nineteen: Do Some Direct Sales

One of the reasons Jerry likes the real estate business so much is that he has direct contact with prospects and clients. He gets the opportunity to make new friends and develop relationships. That's what your group of clients represents: Friends on purpose.

Selling means paying attention to those who have bought from you, understanding their needs and wants, and delivering products and services that take care of those.

Some people say they are selling solutions to problems. We like to think that we are providing something to increase the opportunity for a great lifestyle, a comfortable home, and a high quality of life for our clients.

Part of selling is a matter of tending to our clients' needs and wants. Sometimes it is service oriented. Other times it is problem solving oriented—finding that home that is just right in the perfect location that is also affordable.

Regardless of the mode, our job in direct sales is to ask a lot of questions.

Ask the big three:

➢ What is your current or past agent or broker doing or done for you that you liked? (If you are the current agent this question is about you.)

> What is your current or previous agent doing or done for you that you didn't like? (If you are the current agent you better listen real close to this answer.)

> If you could wave a magic wand, what would you want most from your current agent? (If this isn't you, the answer to this question represents a tremendous opportunity to satisfy this client where your competitor is not.)

These are the only three questions you need to do an effective job in selling your real estate services.

Obviously, you can ask more questions and develop other conversations to extend your relationship, but these three questions are key and can revive or energize any sales effort you have going now.

Strategies to Kick Your Direct Sales Up a Notch:

1)   Make a joint prospecting call with a fellow agent. On one call you do the talking, on another call he or she does the talking, and on the next call, you both do.

2)   Go door-to-door to hand out your favor, your trinket, your athletic schedule, your flag, your magnet, etc. As you do this, also offer your help in terms of real estate. Your competition isn't doing this.

3)   Take someone on your administrative support team on a listing presentation one time and watch the new appreciation within your team.

HIGH IMPACT STRATEGY NUMBER TWENTY: CONSIDER TELEMARKETING

L et's face it, some of us are connected to our telephones a lot. The phone is the essential tool of communication; however, e-mail is quickly catching up.

Calling someone with a prospecting pitch that sounds canned without having permission from the person you are calling is interruptive marketing. It's the same kind of marketing that happens at your home when you are sitting down to dinner. You are interrupted and solicited to buy something you have no interest in whatsoever. That is not what we are suggesting here.

We consider telemarketing as another touch to the client or prospect. We consider it the same as a direct mail postcard, a personal visit, or a handshake at a networking event. You simply need to know what you are going to say. You can find detailed scripts of what to say in any prospecting situation at **www.jpsalessystems.com**.

What benefits are you ready to talk about in sound-byte fashion? What problems are you ready to solve for clients? How do you even know they have those problems?

You can quickly see that asking a lot of questions is important when on the phone. At this point you may be thinking: "How do I know if the person on the other end will be patient enough to listen to my questions and then answer them?"

You don't know, just like you don't know if someone will see you when you visit. You have to put yourself in high probability situations.

This means you must have a lukewarm situation at hand—that your phone calls should be to people you have something in common with.

Maybe that something in common is that you met at a networking session. Maybe you belong to the same Chamber of Commerce or association. Maybe you sit on the same board of directors with the person. These situations are warm. You have a connection; therefore, it is far from being a cold, interruptive type of call.

Exhaust the connections first before ever calling cold. If you exhaust them, maybe you can join another association or attend another networking event to keep the calls as warm as possible for as long as possible.

Avoid cold calling on the telephone as much as possible, as this is the lowest impact way to prospect for business. Only do this when you absolutely have no one else to call. For a detailed list of high impact income producing activities, check out Jerry's book, *Secrets to Real Estate Success*.

Strategies to Kick Your Telemarketing Up a Notch:

1) Write out your script, but don't sound like you're reading it. Practice it so it becomes second nature. Always have your ideas and thoughts planned out.

2) When you leave a voice mail messages, leave tips or something that will prompt a call back. For example, "For more details about home values in your community, call me." Or, "For our new list of tips and techniques that will sell your home fast, give me a call and I will bring them right over."

3) As the primary person in your business, you should call the important clients often. Pick a few that are lower on the list and call at random. You'd be surprised what you might find out and what you might get.

4) Let others hear your approach. They might pick up some technique points that might help them in their efforts.

5) Be creative in your voice mails. Remember you are one of many.

6) Your primary call should be to get referrals, not luck into a listing.

High Impact Strategy Number Twenty-One: Do Some Speaking

In a previous chapter we mentioned that you must establish yourself as an expert, and speaking was one of the ways to do that.

> **Speaking is a great marketing tool. You can do it fairly easily depending on your motive and aggressiveness.**

A number of service organizations in your community need speakers every week. Granted, these aren't paid speaking engagements, but that's okay. Your goal is to market your real estate services, not become a professional speaker.

Typically, these service-oriented groups like to hear about:

➤ What's new.

➤ Trends in the market, both technically and economically.

➤ Support for non-profits or community oriented situations.

➤ Success stories.

➤ Stories of special accomplishment.

➤ Anything unusual.

Most of the time you can find something related to one of these topics in your business.

Pick a topic, give it a title, and outline a twenty minute story related to your topic. You now have a speech you can deliver to your group.

Spend most of your time on your introduction (how you want the head of the organization you're addressing to introduce you to the members before your speech), for this is where your "commercial" is.

Be funny, be entertaining, and be memorable.

Practice alone, with your staff, and with family. The more you practice, the more professional you will look. As a result, you will further your credibility and expert status.

The goal of speaking is to dispense information, to create relationships, and to establish credibility.

If you need help as a speaker or presenter, check out your local chapter of Toastmasters or the National Speakers Association. Both are great organizations that can help you hone your public speaking skills.

Strategies to Kick Your Speaking Up a Notch:

1) Collect business cards from your audience, have a drawing, and give a book away to the winner. Use the names in your database for future marketing or communication.

2) Make your speech interactive. Ask what the current challenges are, what the wishes are, etc. Get the audience involved.

3) Tell stories. Don't be a lecturer; be a story teller.

4) Be entertaining. Open strong with a humorous story and close with one, while delivering your message.

5) Ask for feedback.

6) Offer a chance to contact you later for more questions, more information, and details related to buying and selling real estate.

7) Tell people you are a speaker when they ask you what you do.

HIGH IMPACT STRATEGY NUMBER TWENTY-TWO: DEVELOP MULTIPLE HOOKS

Visit **www.marketingforrealestateprofessionals.com** for a free chapter of the book, *Kick It Up A Notch Marketing – 25 High Impact Marketing Strategies for Real Estate Professionals.*

How did that sound? Would it get you interested if you weren't already reading this?

If it did, then it was a successful hook.

A hook is something to help you get noticed. Your hook might be on a web site, a postcard, a letter, or an advertisement. You can use a hook with any marketing.

> **A hook offer can be free information, a free sample, a free consultation, or anything of value that causes a response from your prospect, client, or visitor.**

Here are some hooks you can view as examples. To see the first two, go to **www.market-for-profits.com**. One hook is a free report on how to instantly add fifty people to your network. The second hook is two free chapters of Al's new book, *Guerrilla Marketing in 30 Days*.

For the third sample, go to **www.jpsalessystems.com**. This hook is for free prospecting scripts you can use for a variety of situations.

These hooks extend our relationship with our web site visitors, and make prospects more interested in our areas of expertise, which ultimately could lead to the purchase of our products and services.

This information is not costly, yet it yields tremendous value to those receiving it. Without these hooks visitors might not spend as much time on the site or read with interest the other information offered. Try it on your next marketing piece.

Strategies to Kick Your Hooks Up a Notch:

1)   Brainstorm ideas on what information you can put into special reports, checklists, top ten lists, etc. that you can offer as a hook.

2)   Take an inventory of your marketing to see where you can place your hook.

3)   Test different hooks on the same vehicle to see which ones generate a higher response rate.

HIGH IMPACT STRATEGY NUMBER TWENTY-THREE: WORK YOUR DATABASE

If you have a list of your clients, their contact information and addresses, you are sitting on a marketing goldmine. Why? Because your best prospect is always a current client.

Those who have bought from you in the past have a high probability of buying from you in the future. They already know you, trust you, have confidence in you, and like you; these are all reasons to buy from you again.

Having these clients in a list allows you to market to them over and over and over. Getting new clients only adds to your list—a.k.a.: your database.

A good database allows you to target your marketing. With your database, you have the ability to sort according to geographic location, whether they are a buyer or a seller, date since last contact, etc.

Sorting allows you to send targeted and customized marketing messages. Targeted marketing is much more effective than mass marketing. With a maintained database and this level of personalization, you can do small mailings that produce higher responses.

Now you can see why a database can be a marketing goldmine!

Believe it or not, but some people still don't keep track of who works with them or contacts them. Not doing this is passing up one of the best marketing weapons you can have.

> **Spend sixty percent of your marketing time and money on current and past clients.**

You can't effectively spend your marketing time and money if you don't know who your past and current clients are.

Spend the remaining of your marketing time and money on prospects. You can buy lists or accumulate permission-based names to market to. This also represents a database.

Keep your databases separate and distinct so as to sort and target appropriately.

Strategies to Kick Your Databases Up a Notch:

1) Capture e-mail addresses when prospects contact you or clients work with you. An e-mail database is also a goldmine, is permission-based, and can be marketed to with great success.

2) Done is better than perfect. Use a simple spreadsheet program to enter and keep track of data if you don't have a purchasing program or point of purchase program for your business.

3) Do a "return service requested" mailing once a year to your database to clean up those names that have moved away or that are no longer valid.

HIGH IMPACT STRATEGY NUMBER TWENTY-FOUR: PRACTICE CLIENT ATTENTION

Many people give their top five or even top ten accounts plenty of attention. These are the people who have listed with them and worked with them over and over and over. They are people you have a relationship with.

Sometimes fighting fires or working on administrative tasks can consume much of our day, and we forget to give our current and past clients "selling attention."

Selling attention does not have to be in the form of a prospecting call. Nor does it have to be in the form of the many listing and selling options we meet about.

> **We must give all clients this attention in order to maintain our top of mind awareness, maintain our good relationships, and be at their service when they need us most.**

We see, too many times, sales professionals hiding behind the phone or hiding behind an e-mail.

Consider hand-delivering offers, returning phone calls with a personal visit, and just showing up for no invited reason. That's "sales attention."

Here are twenty reasons to call on a client. Try them if you're not using them and take it one step beyond…try them on a prospect. You'll be surprised at your results and your new relationships that emerge:

1) Drop off comps to a listing client.

2) Drop off the newest brochure or flyer showing new listings.

3) Deliver free products, i.e. free notepads.

4) Deliver information about lenders, mortgage rates, interior design services, etc.

5) Drop off a premium giveaway or free gift (pens, mouse pads, books, etc.).

6) Deliver an article reprint about your company or authored by you.

7) Deliver a postcard asking them to visit your web site.

8) Drop off the latest press release.

9) Introduce a new employee in person.

10) Introduce client service teams via profiles and printed fact sheets.

11) Deliver the most recent newsletter in person.

12) Introduce your broker.

13) Hand-deliver a contract.

14) Provide good clients tickets to a sports or theatrical event.

15) Share a page of your favorite web site with your client.

16) Deliver an article of interest you found in the media.

17) Deliver a copy of the news where your client appeared.

18) Hand-deliver a thank you note.

19) Present a client appreciation plaque or award.

20) Present a survey to your client.

Many more ideas and reasons to visit a client exist that are not mentioned here. These are just a few ideas that work and that clients appreciate. Also be sure to ask a client how often they would like to hear from you. Client attention is vital, especially during tougher economic times. Remember, your best prospect is a current client.

Strategies to Kick Your Client Attention Up a Notch:

1) What client attention ideas get the most response from your client?

2) Can you create a special event day to show appreciation or attention towards your client? For example, ABC Real Estate Agency Client Appreciation Day.

HIGH IMPACT STRATEGY NUMBER TWENTY-FIVE: GET ACTIVE WITH FUSION MARKETING

W ebster defines fusion as a merging of diverse, distinct, or separate elements into a unified whole. That's exactly what happens when you join with another business to market. That's why this is called fusion marketing.

> **Fusion marketing is nothing more than a strategic alliance with another business. Strategic alliances truly are synergistic.**

Constructing an alliance is easy to do. Anyone can do it; it just takes a little bit of an effort. Don't read this and put it in your briefcase or on the shelf. Act on this information.

We recommend that everyone reading this, regardless of the stage of marketing you are in, regardless of the age of your business, regardless of whether you have done this before or not, set up some type of fusion marketing.

Here is how to set an alliance up:

Step 1

Define a "power partner." A power partner is someone who has similar prospects as you and who could benefit from the same type of prospect. This person is not necessarily in the same business as you, so teaming up is okay.

111

Here are some examples: An attorney and an insurance agent. A printer and a designer. A landscaper and a builder. A real estate agent and a mortgage broker. A network marketer and an entrepreneur. A massage therapist and a chiropractor.

Step 2

Figure out with your power partner what to offer. Maybe the printer gives a two-for-one offer, while the designer offers to design a logo and a direct mail piece. Maybe the attorney offers a free consultation on wills, while the insurance agent offers a tips list on avoiding probate tax. Maybe the massage therapist offers a free midday office visit for a massage break, while the chiropractor offers a nutrition class. Figure out what joint offer makes sense.

Step 3

Write up a general letter of agreement. This doesn't have to be a major league legal document, but the one thing that hinders an alliance is lack of communication. This assures who does what and gets what. It can be a simple e-mail exchange.

Step 4

Package it up. Write marketing copy, a sales letter, press releases if appropriate, e-mail letters, etc. Either you can both write these things up and compare notes, or one person writes them and lets the other approve. Be creative here. Be benefit oriented. What's in it for the prospect?

Step 5

Combine mailing lists and communicate to both sets. Don't worry about who has more or less, just combine them. When two people put their lists together, they both have a list much larger than if each did it alone. You can do this with direct mail or e-mail. Obviously, e-mail is cheaper.

Step 6

Be responsive to any responses. Make it easy to take the next step, and keep track of your results. Follow up to every reply. Your attention will convert prospects into paying clients. Share leads and conversions for future follow up and future marketing.

Step 7

Both parties continue to market to each of the converted people as follow up marketing.

That's all there really is to it. It's a straight set of deliberate, planned out steps, with a high degree of communication and execution. That's what all marketing is. And the more you spell and plan it out, the higher probability someone will act upon it.

Strategies to Kick Your Fusion Marketing Up a Notch:

1)   Brainstorm the types of businesses that are power partners for you.

2)   Identify specific company names that fit the power partner definition.

3)   Create an offer and approach these power partners.

4)   After you start one strategic alliance, start another one.

5)   Do a joint mailing with a company that is similar to yours, like a mortgage company, a home insurance agent, a warranty company, etc.

APPENDIX

A Quick Word About Turbo Charging Your Marketing Efforts

Some of you like this book so much that you want more to help guide your marketing. Both Al and Jerry are very accessible to answer your quick questions whenever you have one. E-mail is the best way to catch them.

Al Lautenslager: **al@market-for-profits.com**

Jerry Pujals: **jerry@jpsalessystems.com**

A QUICK NOTE FROM AL:

I have just the thing for those of you who want to pursue a more aggressive and direct marketing program—in other words a turbo-charger for your marketing or putting your marketing on steroids.

I have Guerrilla Marketing coaching packages available specifically for you. This is done via telephone consultations each week and unlimited e-mails. For more information please visit: **www.market-for-profits.com/set_coaching_gmcoaching.html**.

Because I am a Certified Guerrilla Marketing Coach and co-author, I will even throw in a free copy of my latest book, *Guerrilla Marketing in 30 Days*.

I will be available to keep you on track; help you focus; suggest tips, techniques, and methods; as well as hold you accountable for your planned activity.

Please contact me for a special offer (mention this part of this book).

Thanks for being a fan,

Al Lautenslager
al@market-for-profits.com
www.market-for-profits.com

A QUICK NOTE FROM JERRY:

Nothing gets me more excited than helping real estate agents succeed. That's why I founded JP Sales Systems, Inc.—a real estate training and accountability success firm.

I've spent many years as a mega-producing real estate sales agent and created a sales system that enabled me to regularly sell over 100 homes and earn over a million dollars a year working less than three days a week. Consistently the #1 salesperson in the Northern California market, I knew that others who were dedicated to succeed could apply my system.

To help other real estate agents and their family members, I began to share my system in a no-nonsense coaching program, emphasizing a work-and-fun-in-life balance. Coaching led to workshops and JP Sales Systems' new PAL software, designed to help agents maintain accountability to reach their goals.

My renowned system ranks at the top of the significant contributions to the field of real estate. Today, JP Sales Systems, Inc. offers seminars, workshops, personal coaching, and other professional support programs.

To find out more about all these products and services and how they can increase your level of success in real estate, please visit **www.jpsalessystems.com**.

Here's to your success.

Jerry Pujals

jerry@jpsalessystems.com
www.jpsalessystems.com

SIGN UP FOR "MARKET FOR PROFITS" FREE E-ZINE

Go to this link and sign up today:
www.market-for-profits.com

Be one of the first to benefit from Jerry's new book:
Secrets to Real Estate Success:
Increase Your Efficiency and Profits in 90 Days or Less

Go to this link for more information:
www.jpsalessystems.com

QUICK START ACTION SHEET

What I will do next, starting right now:_____

_____

_____

_____

_____

_____

_____

_____

_____

_____

_____

_____

_____

_____

_____

_____

_____

_____

_____

_____

_____

_____

_____

_____

_____

_____

_____

_____

FREE SPECIAL REPORT #1

Instant Clients! Things to Do to Get a Client Now

Provided courtesy of Al Lautenslager

In tough times, in bountiful times, in whatever kind of times you find yourself in, remember the power of marketing. In fact, as has been pointed out in this book, marketing is not an expense you should cut during tough times. It is an area that deserves more spending and certainly more attention. The reason for this obviously is to grow the revenue side of the income statement, as we all strive for a new breakeven point and beyond.

Many types of marketing programs work. Some are very effective but can be more medium- to long-term. Sometimes, especially in tough times, a business can have the normal patience towards this medium- and long-term time frame. Other times, however, when a business is struggling or when you need increased revenue, you can't devote the proper amount of time that some marketing programs take.

Sometimes a business needs a shot of revenue for a quicker than normal fix. In all of these circumstances, a long and drawn out marketing program and plan is not always the answer. Businesses are looking for more immediate, shorter term results.

Given that scenario, here are five things a business can do today to not only get an order, but also to get a new client. Gaining a client and gaining the business versus just getting an order certainly is more important, especially when calculating the lifetime value of such a client acquisition.

1) Call the local Chamber of Commerce. Sometimes an Area Business Association or other civic organization will work. Ask to speak to the Executive Director, a board member, and/or one committee head. For each one of these three, identify yourself and your company. State your objective as wanting to meet one person within the organization other than him or her to work together with—one person within the organization who may be able to help grow your business. Sometimes a good "power partner" can be identified, i.e. that business partner in a similar industry or service area who shares clients much like yours.

2) Obtain a letter of recommendation from a client in a geographical area. This can be a city, region, or even an office building. Hand-deliver this letter of recommendation with your own letter of introduction to all others in that area. "We're already in your building and that's good for you. We are doing business with ABC Company, who is right in your area; therefore, we can meet with you to discuss your projects and the same benefits that we are offering ABC Company …"

    Sometimes clients are more apt to do business with you when they know you are very accessible and always around. The endorsement from a current client lends tremendous credibility to you as you strive to build the trust and confidence necessary to start doing business with a new client. People like to do business with people they like and know. When that isn't possible, they like to do business with people their friends and associates like and know.

3) Broadcast faxes and broadcast e-mails are effective. Some people don't like broadcast faxes and e-mails and will ask to be unsubscribed to such communication. Please respect these requests. It's no different

than a client you are mailing to asking to be taken off your list. We all will encounter them. It's a fact of our business life and all the marketing we do. Even with that said, broadcast faxes and e-mails can be effective marketing too. You can even go so far as to publish your "privacy policy" on your e-mail or fax communication. It can be as simple as, "We respect your privacy. If for any reason you wish to discontinue receiving these communications, just contact us..."

To your list, send a message offering a free special report or something free related to what you do. Free information always works well, is of value, and can be produced easily. After all, providing value to a client is what you do anyway.

Other questions you can ask when offering free information are: A) Who is the decision maker in any real estate transactions? and B) What is the best time of day to drop off the free information? Once your prospect or client requests that free information, personally deliver the free report or information along with other information on your company's capabilities and offerings. We all know how hard it can be to get in front of the actual decision maker.

Offering free information like this actually is the equivalent to an instant appointment and can be capitalized on instantly.

4) Call someone in an affiliated business and ask to share a prospect, client, lead, or list. Exchange one for one. Some affiliated businesses are listed under "Power Partners."

When two people exchange a dollar bill, they each have a dollar. When they exchange a friend, lead, list, or client, they each then have two friends, leads, lists, or clients. You'd be surprised who will participate with you on this one, especially if you offer mailing services, list acquisition services, and other marketing that your power partner could benefit from.

5) Send letters directly to current clients asking for referrals. This will further support "top-of-mind" awareness with your client. Your best prospect still is a current client. One of the reasons they are your best prospect is because they already know you, trust you, and have confidence in your work. These are the types of benefits they want their friends and associates to have also.

Directly asking them for others who could share in the same benefits that they receive will turn up a few "warm" people to call on. This should be part of an ongoing marketing plan but can work also in the short-term. Some companies have had success with telephone blitzes, using direct referral requests as the basis of the calls.

Sometimes a client has a referral but doesn't think of it until you ask them or remind them of who can best benefit from your services and products.

These are instant, short-term strategies for gaining clients. These have worked when businesses are in trouble, when they're at the bottom of a sales cycle, when businesses want to fill new capacity, and when they just generally want a boost in sales/revenue.

Just like any other marketing program, it has to be targeted, worked, and followed up upon. These short-term actions should be a part of the marketing plan, but not the only part of the plan. Remember, marketing is made up of many, many, many things. These five short-term items are only part of those "many, many things." Planning and organizing these five steps will yield a short-term boost to your client list and a rise in revenue.

For free articles, CD products, marketing products and more information on Al, his services, his company or how to market your business more effectively, visit: **www.market-for-profits.com**

Happy Marketing!

FREE SPECIAL REPORT #2

Want More Real Estate Success? Get Accountable!

Provided courtesy of Jerry Pujals

If you want to be a top producing real estate agent, you must be accountable and have an accountability process in place. While many other factors, mindsets, and habits play into your success level, your level of accountability is the hinge-pin that makes everything else possible.

So, what exactly does accountability mean? The dictionary defines it as the quality or state of being accountable, liable, or responsible. In simpler terms, it means having a system that ensures you do what you said you would do, even when you don't feel like doing it.

Ask yourself, "Who holds you responsible for completing daily tasks that will generate more sales? To whom are you liable if you don't do what you need to do?" For most agents, the answer is "no one."

Independent or Not...Here We Come

The fact is that most real estate agents are not accountable. Why? Because they're independent contractors. They don't have bosses, and that is their detriment.

This flexibility attracts thousands of people to this industry every year. The irony is that this very flexibility is what kills so many careers. Those in the top three percent know how to manage all the freedom; those in the ninety-seven percent do not.

Think about it...as a real estate agent, you can pick up and go anytime you want. You don't have to make a certain number of calls per day to generate leads. You don't have a quota for sales or listings. You don't even have to show up at the office if you don't want to. But when you let one thing slide for too long, such as not prospecting enough or not going on listing appointments, a domino effect starts to occur. When one aspect of your business goes downhill, others quickly follow suit.

So the challenge is getting agents back on task to where they create a schedule, respect it, and work only forty hours per week. If you ask most agents how much they work, they'll tell you they put in sixty or more hours per week. But if you analyze their schedule and look at their income producing activities, you'll quickly see that these same people actually work less than twenty hours per week. The rest of the time they're engaging in non-income producing activities—the "busyness" of real estate—rather than the real business of real estate. And that's a recipe for disaster.

So how do you gain accountability? Consider the following:

Have an Accountability Partner

The first step to accountability is to have an accountability partner. This person holds you to your word. If you say you're going to prospect for four hours each day, your accountability partner ensures you do precisely that...no excuses. If you don't do what you said you would do, or if you deviate from your plan in any way, this person "calls you on the carpet" and makes sure you get back on track. In general, having an accountability partner is the best way to take your well-laid plans and convert them into action.

We all instinctively know who can hold us accountable. Some people in our life agree with everything we say, pat us on the back, and act as our cheerleaders, while others aren't afraid to confront us on important issues. When it comes to an accountability partner, you want someone who is more like the latter. Realize that your cheerleader and accountability partner likely love you the same amount, so this isn't an issue of who loves you more. This is an issue of who will hold your feet to the fire. When it comes to an accountability partner, don't choose the path of least resistance. Choose someone who will confront you when needed—someone who will push you to be your best.

Look at the people in your life. Who are the people who can get "tough" with you? It may be your spouse, your sibling, your broker, your co-worker, your brother-in-law, etc. It may even be someone you don't know that well, such as the guy who works in the office down the hall, a personal trainer you just met, or even a business coach. The key question to ask is: "Will this person push me to be my best, even when it hurts?" If your answer is anything other than a resounding "yes," then keep looking. The last thing you want is an accountability partner who will let you slide.

Form an Accountability Group

Some people prefer to start with an accountability group rather than an accountability partner. Most real estate agents work in an office with several agents. When you have an accountability group, you develop an alliance within your office, where all the agents help each other as a whole, rather than individually. Most brokers are going to be excited about this group forming.

In this group, you get together to share ideas, discuss goals, exchange feedback, give each other motivation, and challenge each other to produce more. For example, as a group, you may decide that every day you are going to show up by 10:00 a.m. and prospect. If someone doesn't show up, the group tries to find out why that person didn't show up and what everyone can do to help him or her show up the next day. Obviously, this one person may simply not want to participate in the group. If so, that's okay. You can't force someone to be accountable. He or she must want to do it.

After being in the group for a while, certain people will naturally gravitate towards each other as accountability partners for more specific items. That's completely normal and part of the process. This does not mean those individuals will leave the group; it simply means they are looking for some more specific accountability items. The purpose of the group is to get the entire office focused on goals and on helping each other, and to introduce the accountability process to people.

To introduce the idea of an accountability group to your office, get the agents together in a meeting. Start the conversation by telling the group some of your challenges—maybe you need help prospecting or role playing. And then find out what challenges other people have. You may find that most people struggle with the same two or three things.

For example, you may say, "You know, I think I could be a lot more efficient if I did more prospecting and role playing, but I sometimes have trouble doing these things. I'd like to find out what things other people here would like to do more often but for some reason don't do them. (Let the group talk.) Great. Now that we each know what would help this office produce more as a group, as well as what would help us all individually, why don't we help each other by creating an accountability group. We will each know what the group needs to do as a whole, and we will work together to make sure we do these things and hold each other accountable for our tasks."

If you keep the meeting positive and focused on the benefit—the fact that the office and each individual agent will produce more—then most groups are easy to form. Getting your broker involved is a good idea too, as brokers often love the idea of an accountability group. Most brokers certainly want their agents to be more productive.

Get Accountable Today

The more accountable you are to your daily tasks and long-term goals, the higher your chances for accomplishing everything you desire. Remember, when it comes to accountability, the path of least resistance is not the ideal road to take. Get in a group setting where you have support from multiple people, or choose an accountability partner who will be tough on you. Yes, accountability hurts sometimes. But as the old saying goes, "No pain, no gain."

What's even better is that as your accountability grows and you do the things you must do on a regular basis, you form a good habit. Your day then doesn't feel complete unless you do the things you want to be accountable for. When that happens, you've pushed through the pain and can enjoy the fruits of your labor without the negative feelings. You'll no longer look at things like prospecting, role playing, or getting into the office on time as chores. They'll be natural parts of your day that you enjoy. When those feelings surface, you can be sure you're on your way to becoming a top producing agent.

For real estate success books, marketing products, personal coaching, free downloads and articles, and more information on Jerry, his services, his company, or how to succeed in real estate beyond your wildest dreams, visit: **www.jpsalessystems.com**

Best of luck in all your real estate pursuits!

About Al Lautenslager

Al Lautenslager, best-selling co-author of *Guerrilla Marketing in 30 Days*, is an award-winning marketing/ public relations consultant, direct mail promotion specialist, author, speaker, and entrepreneur. He is the principal of Market For Profits, a Chicago based marketing consulting firm, and also the president and owner of The Ink Well, a commercial printing and mailing company in Wheaton, IL. He is also the author of *The Ultimate Guide to Direct Marketing* (Entrepreneur Press).

Al is a multiple winner of "business of the year" awards from various organizations. His articles can be seen on over fifty on-line sites. He is also a featured business coach for the online site of Entrepreneur Magazine, **www.entrepreneur.com**. Al is a member of the National Speakers Association.

A member of USA Today's small business panel, and a certified Guerrilla Marketing coach, Al is a much-in-demand speaker on the subject of marketing. Recently, *Fast Company Magazine* announced that Al is a finalist for its annual Fast 50 "ordinary people doing extraordinary things" as "leaders, innovators, and technology pioneers."

Al speaks to audiences wanting to learn more about building their businesses through low or no-cost marketing tactics. Many in his audiences leave with strategies and tactics they can use the same day.

About Jerry Pujals

"Informative." "Uplifting." "Motivating." "Powerful." That's what audience members say about Jerry Pujals—one of today's leading real estate sales trainers and motivational speakers. Consistently ranked in the top one percent of real estate agents nationwide, Jerry coaches and trains some of the nation's top producing agents, showing them how to increase production, efficiency, and quality of life.

A no-nonsense speaker who packs a room, Jerry delivers his message with honesty and real-world experience. He delves deep to the truths of real estate and selling success, and shatters the myths that hold agents and salespeople back. Jerry challenges people to push through any self-limiting beliefs that hinder their progress, and he provides practical tools and techniques people can put into play immediately.

People leave Jerry's workshops with a newfound focus on their career and workable strategies to propel them to the top. Audience members "catch" Jerry's enthusiasm and can-do attitude, to the point that they feel empowered to reach higher sales goals. Both novice and veteran agents learn something new each time they hear Jerry speak.

Jerry is a member of the National Speakers Association, the National Association of Realtors, the California Association of Realtors), the Bay Area Real Estate Information Services, and Toastmasters International. His book, *Secrets to Real Estate Success*, offers insights and strategies for becoming more accountable to reach your real estate goals.

Other books by Al Lautenslager:

Guerrilla Marketing in 30 Days (Entrepreneur Press, February, 2005)
The Ultimate Guide to Direct Marketing (Entrepreneur Press, October, 2005)

Other books by Jerry Pujals:

Secrets to Real Estate Success: Increase Your Efficiency and Profits in 90 Days or Less (Cameo Publications, December 2005)

Jerry Pujals can speak to your group on the following topics:

Take Action: Simple Steps to Real Estate Excellence

Too many real estate agents are working hard but not producing the results they deserve. Sound familiar? You're not alone. If you're tired of watching one or two star performers get all the business, if you're yearning for the secrets to attaining true real estate sales excellence, then this is the workshop for you. Jerry Pujals will show you how to turn your career around and kick it into high gear.

Sales Mastery: How to Close More Deals and Make Money in Real Estate

The only way to make money in real estate is to close sales. Simply knowing real estate procedures is not enough to be successful. You must also know what to say to buyers and sellers, how to generate qualified leads, and how to work your inventory in order to close more deals. Jerry Pujals will show you how to master real estate sales processes so you can increase your income dramatically.

Make It Happen

"The economy is bad." "There's not much inventory right now." "That top producer stole my lead." "We're not getting much walk-in traffic." How many excuses do you make for your lack of real estate success? Now it's time to end the excuses once and for all so you can realize your real estate dreams. Jerry Pujals will show you how to eliminate excuses and replace them with results.

For more information on Jerry's speaking topics, or for a customized topic, please contact him at **jerry@jpsalessystems.com**.

Book Order Form

Fax orders: 843-645-3771. Send this form.

Telephone orders: Call 1-866-37-CAMEO (372-2636) toll free.
Or 843-785-3770 Have your credit card handy.

Secure Online Ordering: www.cameopublications.com

Postal Orders: Cameo Publications, 478 Brown's Cove Road,
Ridgeland, SC 29936, USA.

Kick It Up a Notch Marketing:
25 High Impact Marketing Strategies for Real Estate Professionals
$24.95 US FUNDS $28.32 CAN FUNDS
ISBN: 0-9774659-3-4

 # Books _____ x $ _____ = _____

+ S & H _____
Order Total = _____

Please send more FREE infromation on:

☐ Consulting   ☐ Speaking/Seminar   ☐ Webinars   ☐ other books

Name: _____

Address: _____

City: _____State: ___Zip: _____

Phone:_____ Email(optional): _____

Shipping:
USA: $4.95 for first item; add $2.00 for each additional item
SC residents please include 5% sales tax.

Card #: _____

Name on card: _____ Exp date: _____